The Big Muffin Recipe Book

Easy Recipes for True Muffin Lovers

G000066385

Table of Contents

Introduction

Get ready….it's muffin time! I'm sure you just can't wait to start baking some golden brown beauties and who could blame you, muffins are the absolute best! Luckily, you now have this awesome cookbook that will provide you with tons of delicious muffin recipes that you can make in a flash. Each recipe has been carefully crafted to have the perfect taste and texture while still being fast and easy to make. Sounds like a muffin dream, right?!? Well, you won't be dreaming for long. All you need to do is pick which recipe to make first and you will be enjoying one of the best muffins of your life soon.

I compiled his muffin book in order to share all the delicious muffins I have created over the years. Muffins are one of my all time favorite breakfast foods and I often find myself enjoying them as a mid day snack too- I just can't resist! So, I decided that everyone should be able to have access to these unbeatable recipes and I wrote them all down here, for you! Now every super simple muffin recipe I have found can be your as well and, as I mentions before, you can make them all in under ten minutes! Fresh, homemade muffins, hot out of the oven is the best way to start any day.

The only thing that is tricky about making muffins is deciding what recipe to make first. I always suggest to begin with something simple, something classic, something like a nice chocolate chip muffin. Luckily, there is a delicious chocolate chip muffin recipe in here! Then, move on to something extra healthy like our quinoa muffin or even the Morning Glory muffin. After tackling those two categories, pick anything! Open the book, point and start baking- you really can't go wrong!

So what are you waiting for? Don't you want to eat the most fresh, tasty muffin in the world? Grab a bowl, a spoon and a measuring cup and start baking!! Enjoy.

Blueberry Muffins

Everyone needs a perfect blueberry muffin recipe in their arsenal and this recipe is it. These muffins are simple to make and come out absolutely delicious every time. People will definitely be asking you for your muffin recipe after one bite of these!

Active Time: 10 minutes

Yield: 8 Muffins

Ingredients

- 1/3 cup oil (vegetable, canola or coconut)
- 1/3 cup whole milk
- 1 large egg
- 1 tsp vanilla extract
- ¾ cup sugar
- 2 tsp baking powder
- ½ tsp cinnamon
- 1/8 tsp nutmeg
- 1 ½ cups flour
- ¼ tsp salt
- 1 ½ cups blueberries

Directions

1. In a large bowl, combine the baking powder, sugar, cinnamon, nutmeg, flour and salt. Whisk together well.

2. Add the egg, vanilla, whole milk and oil to the bowl and whisk all the **Ingredients** together until the batter is smooth.

3. Fold in the blueberries.

4. Scoop the muffin batter into a regular sized muffin tin with paper liners, filling each cup about ¾ of the way to the top.

Raspberry Muffins

Warm raspberries in the middle of a sweet muffin is like a baking dream come true. Use fresh or frozen raspberries in this recipe as either will give you perfect, homemade muffin results!

Active Time: 10 minutes

Yield: 8 Muffins

Ingredients

- 1/3 cup oil (vegetable, canola or coconut)
- 1/3 cup whole milk
- 1 large egg
- 1 tsp vanilla extract
- ¾ cup sugar
- 2 tsp baking powder
- ½ tsp cinnamon
- 1/8 tsp nutmeg
- 1 ½ cups flour
- ¼ tsp salt
- 1 ½ cups raspberries

Directions

1. In a large bowl, combine the baking powder, sugar, cinnamon, nutmeg, flour and salt. Whisk together well.

2. Add the egg, vanilla, whole milk and oil to the bowl and whisk all the **Ingredients** together until the batter is smooth.

3. Fold in the raspberries.

4. Scoop the muffin batter into a regular sized muffin tin with paper liners, filling each cup about ¾ of the way to the top.

5. Bake the muffins in a 400 degree F oven for about 20 to 24 minutes. Allow to cool then serve!

6. These muffins will keep for about 3-4 days at room temperature.

Blackberry Muffins

It's not everyday that you will come across a delicious blackberry muffin. However, once you try this recipe, that will definitely change as you will want to make these all the time.

Active Time: 10 minutes

Yield: 8 Muffins

Ingredients

- 1/3 cup oil (vegetable, canola or coconut)
- 1/3 cup whole milk
- 1 large egg

- 1 tsp of vanilla extract
- ¾ cup sugar
- ½ tsp cinnamon
- 1 ½ cups flour
- ¼ tsp salt
- 1 ½ cups blackberries
- 2 tsp of baking powder
- 2 Tbsp powdered sugar

Directions

1. In a large bowl, combine the baking powder, cinnamon, sugar, flour and salt. Whisk together well.

2. Add the egg, vanilla, whole milk and oil to the bowl and whisk all the **Ingredients** together until the batter is smooth.

3. Fold in the blackberries.

4. Scoop the muffin batter into a regular sized muffin tin with paper liners, filling each cup about ¾ of the way to the top.

5. Bake the muffins in a 400 degree F oven for about 20 to 24 minutes. Allow to cool then dust with powdered sugar and serve!

6. These muffins will keep for about 3-4 days at room temperature.

Strawberry Muffins

A good strawberry muffin is like pure gold. These are especially amazing in the beginning of summer when fresh strawberries are everywhere. Biting into a moist strawberry muffin is what summer is all about!

Active Time: 10 minutes

Yield: 8 Muffins

Ingredients

- 1/3 cup oil (vegetable, canola or coconut)
- 1/3 cup whole milk
- 1 large egg
- 1 tsp vanilla extract
- ¾ cup sugar
- 2 tsp baking powder
- ½ tsp cinnamon
- 1/8 tsp nutmeg
- 1 ½ cups flour
- ¼ tsp salt
- 1 ½ cups chopped strawberries

Directions

1. In a large bowl, combine the baking powder, sugar, cinnamon, nutmeg, flour and salt. Whisk together well.

2. Add the egg, vanilla, whole milk and oil to the bowl and whisk all the **Ingredients** together until the batter is smooth.

3. Fold in the chopped strawberries.

4. Scoop the muffin batter into a regular sized muffin tin with paper liners, filling each cup about ¾ of the way to the top.

5. Bake the muffins in a 400 degree F oven for about 20 to 24 minutes. Allow to cool then serve!

6. These muffins will keep for about 3-4 days at room temperature.

Strawberry Almond Muffins

While you might see this muffin and think you are about to eat a delicious strawberry muffin, you will be especially surprised and excited to take a bite and taste rich almonds as well. A classic combination that works wonderfully in a muffin!

Active Time: 10 minutes

Yield: 8 Muffins

Ingredients

- 1/3 cup oil (vegetable, canola or coconut)
- 1/3 cup whole milk
- 1 large egg
- 1 tsp almond extract
- ¾ cup sugar
- 2 tsp baking powder
- ½ tsp cinnamon
- 1/8 tsp nutmeg
- 1 ½ cups flour
- ¼ tsp salt

1 ½ cups chopped strawberries

Directions

1. In a large bowl, combine the baking powder, sugar, cinnamon, nutmeg, flour and salt. Whisk together well.

2. Add the egg, almond extract, whole milk and oil to the bowl and whisk all the **Ingredients** together until the batter is smooth.

3. Fold in the strawberries.

4. Scoop the muffin batter into a regular sized muffin tin with paper liners, filling each cup about ¾ of the way to the top.

5. Bake the muffins in a 400 degree F oven for about 20 to 24 minutes. Allow to cool then serve!

6. These muffins will keep for about 3-4 days at room temperature.

Almond Muffins

These muffins are simple to make and have a straightforward, uncomplicated flavor of almonds. They are fantastic on their own or with butter, jelly or peanut butter spread on them as well. A healthy way to start the day!

Active Time: 10 minutes

Yield: 8 Muffins

Ingredients

- 1/3 cup oil (vegetable, canola or coconut)
- 1/3 cup whole milk

- 1 large egg
- 1 tsp almond extract
- ¾ cup sugar
- 2 tsp baking powder
- ½ tsp baking soda
- ½ tsp cinnamon
- 1/8 tsp nutmeg
- 1 ½ cups almond flour

¼ tsp salt

Directions

1. In a large bowl, combine the baking powder, sugar, cinnamon, nutmeg, almond flour and salt. Whisk together well.

2. Add the egg, almond extract, whole milk and oil to the bowl and whisk all the **Ingredients** together until the batter is smooth.

3. Scoop the muffin batter into a regular sized muffin tin with paper liners, filling each cup about ¾ of the way to the top.

4. Bake the muffins in a 400 degree F oven for about 20 to 24 minutes. Allow to cool then serve!

5. These muffins will keep for about 4-5 days at room temperature.

Almond Crunch Muffins

These muffins are simple to make and have a straightforward, uncomplicated flavor of almonds. They are fantastic on their own or with butter, jelly or peanut butter spread on them as well. A healthy way to start the day!

Active Time: 10 minutes

Yield: 8 Muffins

Ingredients

- 1/3 cup oil (vegetable, canola or coconut)
- 1/3 cup whole milk

- 1 large egg
- 1 tsp almond extract
- ¾ cup sugar
- 2 tsp baking powder
- ½ tsp baking soda
- ½ tsp cinnamon
- 1/8 tsp nutmeg
- 1 ½ cups almond flour
- ¼ tsp salt
- 1 cup slivered almonds

Directions

1. In a large bowl, combine the baking powder, sugar, cinnamon, nutmeg, almond flour and salt. Whisk together well.

2. Add the egg, almond extract, whole milk and oil to the bowl and whisk all the **Ingredients** together until the batter is smooth.

3. Fold in the slivered almonds

4. Scoop the muffin batter into a regular sized muffin tin with paper liners, filling each cup about ¾ of the way to the top.

5. Bake the muffins in a 400 degree F oven for about 20 to 24 minutes. Allow to cool then serve!

6. These muffins will keep for about 4-5 days at room temperature.

Peanut Butter Muffins

This muffin is dense with flavor and will fill you up in the morning. While they are easy to make, they are just as easy to eat and will disappear quickly!

Active Time: 10 minutes

Yield: 8 Muffins

Ingredients

- 1/3 cup peanut butter
- 1/3 cup whole milk
- 2 tsp of baking powder
- 1 large egg

- 1 tsp vanilla extract
- ¾ cup sugar
- ½ tsp of cinnamon
- 1 ½ cups flour
- ¼ tsp salt

Directions

1. In a large bowl, combine the baking powder, sugar, cinnamon, flour and salt. Whisk together well.

2. Add the egg, vanilla, whole milk and peanut butter to the bowl and whisk all the **Ingredients** together until the batter is smooth.

3. Scoop the muffin batter into a regular sized muffin tin with paper liners, filling each cup about ¾ of the way to the top.

4. Bake the muffins in a 400 degree F oven for about 20 to 24 minutes. Allow to cool then serve!

5. These muffins will keep for about 3-4 days at room temperature.

Peanut Butter Banana Muffins

A classic peanut butter and banana combo is what makes this muffin truly amazing. They are also vegan which means

Active Time: 10 minutes

Yield: 8 Muffins

Ingredients

- 1/3 cup peanut butter
- 1/3 cup almond milk
- 1 large banana, mashed

- 1 tsp vanilla extract
- ¾ cup sugar
- 2 tsp baking powder
- ½ tsp cinnamon
- 1 ½ cups flour
- ¼ tsp salt

Directions

1. In a large bowl, combine the baking powder, sugar, cinnamon, flour and salt. Whisk together well.

2. Add the mashed banana, vanilla, almond milk and peanut butter to the bowl and whisk all the **Ingredients** together until the batter is smooth.

3. Scoop the muffin batter into a regular sized muffin tin with paper liners, filling each cup about ¾ of the way to the top.

4. Bake the muffins in a 400 degree F oven for about 20 to 24 minutes. Allow to cool then serve!

5. These muffins will keep for about 3-4 days at room temperature.

Peanut Butter Chocolate Chip Muffins

Talk about a delicious muffin! The rich taste of peanut butter pairs perfectly with the mini chocolate chips making this a breakfast that will definitely get you out of bed in the morning!

Active Time: 10 minutes

Yield: 8 Muffins

Ingredients

- 1/3 cup peanut butter
- 1/3 cup whole milk
- 1 large egg

- 1 tsp of vanilla extract
- ¾ cup sugar
- ½ tsp cinnamon
- 1 ½ cups flour
- ¼ tsp salt
- 2 tsp of baking powder
- 1 ½ cups mini chocolate chips

Directions

1. In a large bowl, combine the baking powder, sugar, cinnamon, flour and salt. Whisk together well.

2. Add the egg, vanilla, whole milk and peanut butter to the bowl and whisk all the **Ingredients** together until the batter is smooth.

3. Fold in the chocolate chips

4. Scoop the muffin batter into a regular sized muffin tin with paper liners, filling each cup about ¾ of the way to the top.

5. Bake the muffins in a 400 degree F oven for about 20 to 24 minutes. Allow to cool then serve!

6. These muffins will keep for about 4-5 days at room temperature.

Chocolate Chips Muffins

Sometimes, muffins just need a little something sweet to make them amazing. Chocolate is just the thing! This traditional muffin is perfect for any day, anytime of year!

Active Time: 10 minutes

Yield: 8 Muffins

Ingredients

- 1/3 cup oil (vegetable, canola or coconut)
- 1/3 cup whole milk

- 1 large egg
- 1 tsp vanilla extract
- ¾ cup sugar
- 2 tsp baking powder
- ½ tsp cinnamon
- 1/8 tsp nutmeg
- 1 ½ cups flour
- ¼ tsp salt
- 1 ½ cups chocolate chips

Directions

1. In a large bowl, combine the baking powder, sugar, cinnamon, nutmeg, flour and salt. Whisk together well.

2. Add the egg, vanilla, whole milk and oil to the bowl and whisk all the **Ingredients** together until the batter is smooth.

3. Fold in the chocolate chips.

4. Scoop the muffin batter into a regular sized muffin tin with paper liners, filling each cup about ¾ of the way to the top.

5. Bake the muffins in a 400 degree F oven for about 20 to 24 minutes. Allow to cool then serve!

6. These muffins will keep for about 3-4 days at room temperature.

Oatmeal Raisin Muffins

These muffins are a healthy option for breakfast that you will surely love. They are full of rolled oats which means lots of fiber and energy. The sweet raisins are a nice touch and make this muffin reminiscent of oatmeal raisin cookies.

Active Time: 10 minutes

Yield: 8 Muffins

Ingredients

- 1/3 cup oil (vegetable, canola or coconut)
- 1/3 cup whole milk

- 1 large egg
- 1 tsp vanilla extract
- 1/2 cup honey
- 2 tsp baking powder
- ½ tsp cinnamon
- 1/8 tsp nutmeg
- 1 cup rolled oats
- ½ cups flour
- ¼ tsp salt
- 1 ½ cups raisins

Directions

1. In a large bowl, combine the baking powder, cinnamon, nutmeg, oats, flour and salt. Whisk together well.

2. Add the egg, vanilla, honey, whole milk and oil to the bowl and whisk all the **Ingredients** together until the batter is smooth.

3. Fold in the raisins.

4. Scoop the muffin batter into a regular sized muffin tin with paper liners, filling each cup about ¾ of the way to the top.

5. Bake the muffins in a 400 degree F oven for about 20 to 24 minutes. Allow to cool then serve!

6. These muffins will keep for about 4-5 days at room temperature.

Oatmeal Walnut Muffins

If you are looking for a healthy muffin, look no further- this is it! Walnut flour (finely ground walnuts) makes these muffins dense and filling while also tasty and healthy.

Active Time: 10 minutes

Yield: 8 Muffins

Ingredients

- 1/3 cup oil (vegetable, canola or coconut)
- 1/3 cup whole milk
- 1 large egg
- 1 tsp vanilla extract

- 1/2 cup honey
- 2 tsp baking powder
- ½ tsp cinnamon
- 1/8 tsp nutmeg
- 1 cup rolled oats
- ½ cups walnut flour
- ¼ tsp salt

Directions

1. In a large bowl, combine the baking powder, cinnamon, nutmeg, oats, walnut flour and salt. Whisk together well.

2. Add the egg, vanilla, honey, whole milk and oil to the bowl and whisk all the **Ingredients** together until the batter is smooth.

3. Scoop the muffin batter into a regular sized muffin tin with paper liners, filling each cup about ¾ of the way to the top.

4. Bake the muffins in a 400 degree F oven for about 20 to 24 minutes. Allow to cool then serve!

5. These muffins will keep for about 4-5 days at room temperature.

Oatmeal Chocolate Chip Muffins

A little healthy and a little decadent- what could be better?! Chocolate and oats are a great combo and you don't need to feel bad about eating a few of these beautiful muffins as they are full of healthy fiber!

Active Time: 10 minutes

Yield: 8 Muffins

Ingredients

- 1/3 cup oil (vegetable, canola or coconut)
- 1/3 cup whole milk
- 1 large egg
- 1 tsp vanilla extract
- 1/2 cup honey
- 2 tsp baking powder
- ½ tsp cinnamon
- 1/8 tsp nutmeg
- 1 cup rolled oats
- ½ cups flour
- ¼ tsp salt

1 ½ cups chocolate chips

Directions

1. In a large bowl, combine the baking powder, cinnamon, nutmeg, oats, flour and salt. Whisk together well.

2. Add the egg, vanilla, honey, whole milk and oil to the bowl and whisk all the **Ingredients** together until the batter is smooth.

3. Fold in the chocolate chips.

4. Scoop the muffin batter into a regular sized muffin tin with paper liners, filling each cup about ¾ of the way to the top.

5. Bake the muffins in a 400 degree F oven for about 20 to 24 minutes. Allow to cool then serve!

6. These muffins will keep for about 4-5 days at room temperature.

Apple Cinnamon Muffins

These muffins scream of fall when apples are ripe on the trees and the weather is just beginning to cool down. However, you can definitely make them any time of year as they are tasty no matter wat the season!

Active Time: 10 minutes

Yield: 8 Muffins

Ingredients

- 1/3 cup oil (vegetable, canola or coconut)
- ¼ cup whole milk

- ¼ cup applesauce
- 1 tsp vanilla extract
- ¾ cup sugar
- 2 tsp baking powder
- ¾ tsp cinnamon
- 1/8 tsp nutmeg
- 1 ½ cups flour
- ¼ tsp salt
- 1 cup chopped apples

Directions

1. In a large bowl, combine the baking powder, sugar, cinnamon, nutmeg, flour and salt. Whisk together well.

2. Add the applesauce, vanilla, whole milk and oil to the bowl and whisk all the **Ingredients** together until the batter is smooth.

3. Fold in the chopped apples.

4. Scoop the muffin batter into a regular sized muffin tin with paper liners, filling each cup about ¾ of the way to the top.

5. Bake the muffins in a 400 degree F oven for about 20 to 24 minutes. Allow to cool then serve!

6. These muffins will keep for about 3-4 days at room temperature.

Carrot Cake Muffins

While these muffins may taste like cake, they are actually a healthy breakfast option as they are full of carrots and oats. Talk about the best way to eat vegetables for breakfast!

Active Time: 10 minutes

Yield: 8 Muffins

Ingredients

- 1/3 cup oil (vegetable, canola or coconut)
- ½ cup grated carrot

- 1 large egg
- 1 tsp vanilla extract
- ¾ cup sugar
- 2 tsp baking powder
- ½ tsp cinnamon
- 1/8 tsp nutmeg
- 1 cup flour
- ½ cup rolled oats
- ¼ tsp salt

Directions

1. In a large bowl, combine the baking powder, sugar, cinnamon, nutmeg, oats, flour and salt. Whisk together well.

2. Add the egg, vanilla, carrot and oil to the bowl and whisk all the **Ingredients** together until the batter is smooth.

3. Scoop the muffin batter into a regular sized muffin tin with paper liners, filling each cup about ¾ of the way to the top.

4. Bake the muffins in a 400 degree F oven for about 20 to 24 minutes. Allow to cool then serve!

5. These muffins will keep for about 3-4 days at room temperature.

Morning Glory Muffins

This muffin is a health food addicts favorite. It is full of beneficial **Ingredients** like oats, carrots and walnuts but it also tastes amazing. It is clear why people go crazy for this muffin flavor!

Active Time: 10 minutes

Yield: 8 Muffins

Ingredients

- 1/3 cup oil (vegetable, canola or coconut)
- ½ cup grated carrot
- 1 large egg
- 1 tsp vanilla extract
- ½ cup honey
- 2 tsp baking powder
- ½ tsp cinnamon
- 1/8 tsp nutmeg
- 1 cup flour
- ½ cup rolled oats
- ¼ tsp salt
- ½ cup walnuts, chopped

Directions

1. In a large bowl, combine the oats, baking powder, cinnamon, nutmeg, oats, flour and salt. Whisk together well.

2. Add the egg, honey, vanilla, carrot and oil to the bowl and whisk all the **Ingredients** together until the batter is smooth.

3. Fold in the chopped walnuts.

4. Scoop the muffin batter into a regular sized muffin tin with paper liners, filling each cup about ¾ of the way to the top.

5. Bake the muffins in a 400 degree F oven for about 20 to 24 minutes. Allow to cool then serve!

6. These muffins will keep for about 3-4 days at room temperature.

Snowball Muffins

While these muffins may look like a snowball, they will remind you of a tropical island with their warm, coconut taste. Simple, classic and amazingly tasty, these muffins are a total win!

Active Time: 10 minutes

Yield: 8 Muffins

Ingredients

- 1/3 cup oil (vegetable, canola or coconut)
- 1/3 cup whole milk
- 1 large egg
- 1 tsp vanilla extract
- ¾ cup sugar
- 2 tsp baking powder
- ½ tsp cinnamon
- 1/8 tsp nutmeg
- 1 ½ cups flour
- ¼ tsp salt
- 1 ½ cups shredded coconut, unsweetened
- 2 Tbsp honey

Directions

1. In a large bowl, combine the baking powder, sugar, 1 cup shredded coconut, cinnamon, nutmeg, flour and salt. Whisk together well.

2. Add the egg, vanilla, whole milk and oil to the bowl and whisk all the **Ingredients** together until the batter is smooth.

3. Scoop the muffin batter into a regular sized muffin tin with paper liners, filling each cup about ¾ of the way to the top.

4. Bake the muffins in a 400 degree F oven for about 20 to 24 minutes. Allow to cool then spread the honey across the top of each muffin. Dip each muffin top in the remaining shredded coconut and serve.

5. These muffins will keep for about 3-4 days at room temperature.

Pina Colada Muffins

Want to take a mini vacation every morning? Then make these pina colada muffins! One bite and you will be transported to a tropical island…sounds amazing.

Active Time: 10 minutes

Yield: 8 Muffins

Ingredients

- 1/3 cup oil (vegetable, canola or coconut)
- 1/3 cup whole milk
- 1 large egg

- 1 tsp rum extract
- ¾ cup sugar
- 2 tsp baking powder
- ½ tsp cinnamon
- 1/8 tsp nutmeg
- 1 ½ cups flour
- ¼ tsp salt
- 1 cups shredded coconut, unsweetened
- 1 cups chopped fresh pineapple

Directions

1. In a large bowl, combine the baking powder, sugar, shredded coconut, cinnamon, nutmeg, flour and salt. Whisk together well.

2. Add the egg, rum extract, whole milk and oil to the bowl and whisk all the **Ingredients** together until the batter is smooth.

3. Fold in the fresh chopped pineapple.

4. Scoop the muffin batter into a regular sized muffin tin with paper liners, filling each cup about ¾ of the way to the top.

5. Bake the muffins in a 400 degree F oven for about 20 to 24 minutes. Allow to cool then serve.

6. These muffins will keep for about 3-4 days at room temperature.

Coconut Chocolate Chip

This muffin recipe will quickly become one of your favorites as you taste the amazing flavors of coconut paired with chocolate. Tropical yet rich, dessert like but good for breakfast- this muffin recipe has it all!

Active Time: 10 minutes

Yield: 8 Muffins

Ingredients

- 1/3 cup oil (vegetable, canola or coconut)
- 1/3 cup whole milk
- 1 large egg
- 1 tsp vanilla extract
- ¾ cup sugar
- 2 tsp baking powder
- ½ tsp cinnamon
- 1/8 tsp nutmeg
- 1 ½ cups flour
- ¼ tsp salt
- 1 ½ cups shredded coconut, unsweetened
- 2 Tbsp honey

Directions

1. In a large bowl, combine the baking powder, sugar, 1 cup shredded coconut, cinnamon, nutmeg, flour and salt. Whisk together well.

2. Add the egg, vanilla, whole milk and oil to the bowl and whisk all the **Ingredients** together until the batter is smooth.

3. Scoop the muffin batter into a regular sized muffin tin with paper liners, filling each cup about ¾ of the way to the top.

4. Bake the muffins in a 400 degree F oven for about 20 to 24 minutes. Allow to cool then spread the honey across the top of each muffin. Dip each muffin top in the remaining shredded coconut and serve.

5. These muffins will keep for about 3-4 days at room temperature.

Zucchini Muffins

Looking for a way to put some veggies into your breakfast? Look no further! This recipe for zucchini muffins is outstanding and you will never be able to tell that they are actually healthy too!

Active Time: 10 minutes

Yield: 8 Muffins

Ingredients

- ¼ cup oil
- 1 cup grated zucchini
- 1 large egg
- 1 tsp of vanilla extract
- ¾ cup sugar
- ½ tsp cinnamon
- 1/8 tsp nutmeg
- 1 cup flour
- ½ cup rolled oats
- 2 tsp of baking powder
- ¼ tsp salt

Directions

1. In a large bowl, combine the baking powder, sugar, cinnamon, nutmeg, oats, flour and salt. Whisk together well.

2. Add the egg, vanilla, zucchini and oil to the bowl and whisk all the **Ingredients** together until the batter is smooth.

3. Scoop the muffin batter into a regular sized muffin tin with paper liners, filling each cup about ¾ of the way to the top.

4. Bake the muffins in a 400 degree F oven for about 20 to 24 minutes. Allow to cool then serve!

5. These muffins will keep for about 4-5 days at room temperature.

Chocolate Chip Zucchini Muffins

Sweet and savory muffins are always exciting and this zucchini chocolate chip combo is no different. Rich chocolate and smooth zucchini make for a breakfast treat you will want every day.

Active Time: 10 minutes

Yield: 12 Muffins

Ingredients

- ¼ cup oil
- 1 cup grated zucchini
- 1 large egg
- 1 tsp vanilla extract
- ¾ cup sugar
- 2 tsp baking powder
- ½ tsp cinnamon
- 1/8 tsp nutmeg
- 1 cup flour
- ½ cup rolled oats
- ¼ tsp salt
- ¾ cup chocolate chips

Directions

1. In a large bowl, combine the baking powder, sugar, cinnamon, nutmeg, oats, flour and salt. Whisk together well.

2. Add the egg, vanilla, zucchini and oil to the bowl and whisk all the **Ingredients** together until the batter is smooth.

3. Fold in the chocolate chips.

4. Scoop the muffin batter into a regular sized muffin tin with paper liners, filling each cup about ¾ of the way to the top.

5. Bake the muffins in a 400 degree F oven for about 20 to 24 minutes. Allow to cool then serve!

6. These muffins will keep for about 4-5 days at room temperature.

Apple Zucchini Muffins

Fruit and veggies are combined into one fantastic muffin in this easy recipe. Be sure to use good, crunchy baking apples as they work best in this muffin!

Active Time: 15 minutes

Yield: 12 Muffins

Ingredients

- ¼ cup oil
- 1 cup grated zucchini
- 1 large egg

- 1 tsp vanilla extract
- ¾ cup sugar
- 2 tsp baking powder
- ½ tsp cinnamon
- 1/8 tsp nutmeg
- 1 cup flour
- ½ cup rolled oats
- ¼ tsp salt
- 1 cup chopped apples

Directions

1. In a large bowl, combine the baking powder, sugar, cinnamon, nutmeg, oats, flour and salt. Whisk together well.

2. Add the egg, vanilla, zucchini and oil to the bowl and whisk all the **Ingredients** together until the batter is smooth.

3. Fold in the apple pieces.

4. Scoop the muffin batter into a regular sized muffin tin with paper liners, filling each cup about ¾ of the way to the top.

5. Bake the muffins in a 400 degree F oven for about 20 to 24 minutes. Allow to cool then serve!

6. These muffins will keep for about 4-5 days at room temperature.

Quinoa Muffins

If you want a muffin that is loaded with health benefits, this is the one! These quinoa muffins are made with a natural grain that is healthy and also tastes great.

Active Time: 10 minutes

Yield: 8 Muffins

Ingredients

- 1/3 cup oil (vegetable, canola or coconut)
- 1/3 cup whole milk

- 1 large egg
- 1 tsp vanilla extract
- ¾ cup sugar
- 2 tsp baking powder
- ½ tsp cinnamon
- 1/8 tsp nutmeg
- ¾ cups flour
- ¾ cup ground quinoa
- ¼ tsp salt
- 1 ½ cups chocolate chips

Directions

1. In a large bowl, combine the baking powder, sugar, quinoa, cinnamon, nutmeg, flour and salt. Whisk together well.

2. Add the egg, vanilla, whole milk and oil to the bowl and whisk all the **Ingredients** together until the batter is smooth.

3. Fold in the chocolate chips.

4. Scoop the muffin batter into a regular sized muffin tin with paper liners, filling each cup about ¾ of the way to the top.

5. Bake the muffins in a 400 degree F oven for about 20 to 24 minutes. Allow to cool then serve!

6. These muffins will keep for about 3-4 days at room temperature.

Almond Poppy Seed Muffins

The rich taste of almonds is paired with the nutty taste of poppy seeds to make a truly unique muffin. You will love this new comb and reach for one of these muffins every morning (if they are still around!).

Active Time: 10 minutes

Yield: 8 Muffins

Ingredients

- 1/3 cup oil (vegetable, canola or coconut)
- 1/3 cup whole milk

- 1 large egg
- 1 tsp almond extract
- ¾ cup sugar
- 2 tsp baking powder
- ½ tsp baking soda
- ½ tsp cinnamon
- 1/8 tsp nutmeg
- ½ cups almond flour
- 1 cup flour
- ¼ tsp salt
- ¼ cup poppy seeds

Directions

1. In a large bowl, combine the baking powder, sugar, cinnamon, nutmeg, flour, almond flour and salt. Whisk together well.

2. Add the egg, almond extract, whole milk and oil to the bowl and whisk all the **Ingredients** together until the batter is smooth.

3. Scoop the muffin batter into a regular sized muffin tin with paper liners, filling each cup about ¾ of the way to the top.

4. Bake the muffins in a 400 degree F oven for about 20 to 24 minutes. Allow to cool then serve!

5. These muffins will keep for about 4-5 days at room temperature.

Lemon Poppy Seed Muffins

Lemon poppy seed muffins are a very common flavor and we know why- they taste great! You will love these easy, delicious muffins which are perfect to pop in your mouth when you are on the go in the morning.

Active Time: 10 minutes

Yield: 8 Muffins

Ingredients

- 1/3 cup oil (vegetable, canola or coconut)
- 1/3 cup whole milk
- 1 large egg
- 1 Tbsp lemon juice
- 1 tsp lemon zest
- ¾ cup sugar
- 2 tsp baking powder
- ½ tsp baking soda
- ½ tsp cinnamon
- 1/8 tsp nutmeg
- 1 ½ cups flour
- ¼ tsp salt
- ¼ cup poppy seeds

Directions

1. In a large bowl, combine the baking powder, sugar, cinnamon, poppy seeds, nutmeg, flour, and salt. Whisk together well.

2. Add the egg, lemon juice, lemon zest, whole milk and oil to the bowl and whisk all the **Ingredients** together until the batter is smooth.

3. Scoop the muffin batter into a regular sized muffin tin with paper liners, filling each cup about ¾ of the way to the top.

4. Bake the muffins in a 400 degree F oven for about 20 to 24 minutes. Allow to cool then serve!

5. These muffins will keep for about 4-5 days at room temperature.

Lemon Muffins

Simple and delicious, these muffins are just ideal. They are great for a light tea or an afternoon lunch. Of course, they are also perfect for breakfast!

Active Time: 10 minutes

Yield: 8 Muffins

Ingredients

- 1/3 cup oil (vegetable, canola or coconut)
- 1/3 cup whole milk
- 1 large egg

- 1 Tbsp lemon juice
- 1 tsp lemon zest
- ¾ cup sugar
- 2 tsp baking powder
- ½ tsp baking soda
- ½ tsp cinnamon
- 1/8 tsp nutmeg
- 1 ½ cups flour
- ¼ tsp salt

Directions

1. In a large bowl, combine the baking powder, sugar, cinnamon, nutmeg, flour, and salt. Whisk together well.

2. Add the egg, lemon juice, lemon zest, whole milk and oil to the bowl and whisk all the **Ingredients** together until the batter is smooth.

3. Scoop the muffin batter into a regular sized muffin tin with paper liners, filling each cup about ¾ of the way to the top.

4. Bake the muffins in a 400 degree F oven for about 20 to 24 minutes. Allow to cool then serve!

5. These muffins will keep for about 4-5 days at room temperature.

Strawberry Lemonade Muffins

Sweet strawberries and tangy lemons come together to make a perfect muffin that you won't be able to resist! A perfect summertime treat.

Active Time: 10 minutes

Yield: 8 Muffins

Ingredients

- 1/3 cup oil (vegetable, canola or coconut)
- 1/3 cup whole milk
- 1 large egg
- 1 Tbsp lemon juice
- 1 tsp lemon zest
- ¾ cup sugar
- 2 tsp baking powder
- ½ tsp baking soda
- 1 ½ cups flour
- ¼ tsp salt
- 1 ½ cups chopped strawberries

Directions

1. In a large bowl, combine the baking powder, sugar, flour, and salt. Whisk together well.

2. Add the egg, lemon juice, lemon zest, whole milk and oil to the bowl and whisk all the **Ingredients** together until the batter is smooth.

3. Fold in the strawberries.

4. Scoop the muffin batter into a regular sized muffin tin with paper liners, filling each cup about ¾ of the way to the top.

5. Bake the muffins in a 400 degree F oven for about 20 to 24 minutes. Allow to cool then serve!

6. These muffins will keep for about 4-5 days at room temperature.

Blackberry, Almond and Lemon Muffins

Looking for a new and exciting muffin? Here it is! All the flavors that are packed into this treat are just unbeatable. You will definitely need to eat more than one!

Active Time: 10 minutes

Yield: 12 Muffins

Ingredients

- 1/3 cup oil (vegetable, canola or coconut)
- 1/3 cup whole milk
- 1 large egg
- 1 Tbsp lemon juice
- 1 tsp almond extract
- 1 tsp lemon zest
- ¾ cup sugar
- 2 tsp baking powder
- ½ tsp baking soda
- 1 3/4 cups flour
- ¼ tsp salt
- 1 ½ cups blackberries
- 2 Tbsp powdered sugar

Directions

1. In a large bowl, combine the baking powder, sugar, flour, and salt. Whisk together well.

2. Add the egg, lemon juice, lemon zest, almond extract whole milk and oil to the bowl and whisk all the **Ingredients** together until the batter is smooth.

3. Fold in the blackberries.

4. Scoop the muffin batter into a regular sized muffin tin with paper liners, filling each cup about ¾ of the way to the top.

5. Bake the muffins in a 400 degree F oven for about 20 to 24 minutes. Allow to cool then dust with the powdered sugar and serve!

6. These muffins will keep for about 4-5 days at room temperature.

Peach Yogurt Muffins

The tang of yogurt is the perfect complement for the sweet peaches in this recipe. If you love anything that is preaches and cream flavored, you will love these muffins!

Active Time: 10 minutes

Yield: 12 Muffins

Ingredients

- 1/3 cup oil (vegetable, canola or coconut)
- 1/3 cup whole milk
- ¼ cup plain yogurt

- 1 tsp vanilla extract
- ¾ cup sugar
- 2 tsp baking powder
- 1 ½ cups flour
- ¼ tsp salt
- 1 ½ cups chopped peaches

Directions

1. In a large bowl, combine the baking powder, sugar, flour and salt. Whisk together well.

2. Add the yogurt, vanilla, whole milk and oil to the bowl and whisk all the **Ingredients** together until the batter is smooth.

3. Fold in the peaches.

4. Scoop the muffin batter into a regular sized muffin tin with paper liners, filling each cup about ¾ of the way to the top.

5. Bake the muffins in a 400 degree F oven for about 20 to 24 minutes. Allow to cool then serve!

6. These muffins will keep for about 3-4 days at room temperature.

Printed in Great Britain
by Amazon

53867951R00054